CHINESE ASTROLOGY

The Diagram Group

BROCKHAMPTON
DIAGRAM
GUIDES

Chinese Astrology

First published in Great Britain in 1997 by
Brockhampton Press Ltd
20 Bloomsbury Street
London
WC1 2QA
a member of the Hodder Headline Group PLC

ISBN 1-86019-810-4

Also in this series:
Boxing Skills
Calligraphy
Card Games
Drawing People
How the Body Works
Identifying Architecture
Kings and Queens of Britain
Magic Tricks
Origami
Party Games
Pub Games
SAS Survival Skills
Soccer Skills
Understanding Heraldry
World History

Introduction

Chinese Astrology is an introduction to one of the most ancient of Chinese philosophies which is becoming increasingly popular in the West. The origin of the 12 animal signs is unclear. Legend has it that Buddha (c.563–c. 483 BC) invited all the animals to visit him but only 12 turned up. To thank them he dedicated a year to each animal in the order in which they arrived, so the cycle of animals, based on the lunar year, is repeated every 12 years.

Contents

Finding your animal sign

The animal signs are the most basic aspect of Chinese astrology. The signs are not based on the position of the stars as in Western astrology, but instead on the person's year of birth. Each animal is allocated its own years. There are 12 animals and they always appear in the same order (rat, ox, tiger, rabbit, dragon, snake, horse, goat, monkey, rooster, dog and pig). The cycle of animals, therefore, repeats itself every 12 years.

The Chinese calendar is based on the lunar year (orbits of the Moon around the Earth). The Western calendar is based on the solar year (orbit of the Earth around the Sun). The two do not correspond exactly. Each lunar year, therefore, begins on a slightly different date of the solar year.

To find your animal sign, look up the year of your birth in the first column of the following tables. If you were born in January or February of that year, however, remember to check the dates that the Chinese lunar

31 January 1900 – 17 February 1912

1900	31 January 1900	– 18 February 1901	**RAT**
1901	19 February 1901	– 7 February 1902	**OX**
1902	8 February 1902	– 28 January 1903	**TIGER**
1903	29 January 1903	– 15 February 1904	**RABBIT**
1904	16 February 1904	– 3 February 1905	**DRAGON**
1905	4 February 1905	– 24 January 1906	**SNAKE**
1906	25 January 1906	– 12 February 1907	**HORSE**
1907	13 February 1907	– 1 February 1908	**GOAT**
1908	2 February 1908	– 21 January 1909	**MONKEY**
1909	22 January 1909	– 9 February 1910	**ROOSTER**
1910	10 February 1910	– 29 January 1911	**DOG**
1911	30 January 1911	– 17 February 1912	**PIG**

year begins on as you may find that you actually belong to the previous animal year. Once you have identified your animal sign, read the chapter devoted to that animal.

18 February 1912 – 4 February 1924

1912	18 February	1912 –	5 February	1913	**RAT**
1913	6 February	1913 – 25	January	1914	**OX**
1914	26 January	1914 – 13	February	1915	**TIGER**
1915	14 February	1915 –	2 February	1916	**RABBIT**
1916	3 February	1916 – 22	January	1917	**DRAGON**
1917	23 January	1917 – 10	February	1918	**SNAKE**
1918	11 February	1918 – 31	January	1919	**HORSE**
1919	1 February	1919 – 19	February	1920	**GOAT**
1920	20 February	1920 –	7 February	1921	**MONKEY**
1921	8 February	1921 – 27	January	1922	**ROOSTER**
1922	28 January	1922 – 15	February	1923	**DOG**
1923	16 February	1923 –	4 February	1924	**PIG**

5 February 1924 – 23 January 1936

1924	5 February	1924 – 24	January	1925	**RAT**
1925	25 January	1925 – 12	February	1926	**OX**
1926	13 February	1926 –	1 February	1927	**TIGER**
1927	2 February	1927 – 22	January	1928	**RABBIT**
1928	23 January	1928 –	9 February	1929	**DRAGON**
1929	10 February	1929 – 29	January	1930	**SNAKE**
1930	30 January	1930 – 16	February	1931	**HORSE**
1931	17 February	1931 –	5 February	1932	**GOAT**
1932	6 February	1932 – 25	January	1933	**MONKEY**
1933	26 January	1933 – 13	February	1934	**ROOSTER**
1934	14 February	1934 –	3 February	1935	**DOG**
1935	4 February	1935 – 23	January	1936	**PIG**

24 January 1936 – 9 February 1948

1936	24 January	1936 – 10 February	1937 **RAT**
1937	11 February	1937 – 30 January	1938 **OX**
1938	31 January	1938 – 18 February	1939 **TIGER**
1939	19 February	1939 – 7 February	1940 **RABBIT**
1940	8 February	1940 – 26 January	1941 **DRAGON**
1941	27 January	1941 – 14 February	1942 **SNAKE**
1942	15 February	1942 – 4 February	1943 **HORSE**
1943	5 February	1943 – 24 January	1944 **GOAT**
1944	25 January	1944 – 12 February	1945 **MONKEY**
1945	13 February	1945 – 1 February	1946 **ROOSTER**
1946	2 February	1946 – 21 January	1947 **DOG**
1947	22 January	1947 – 9 February	1948 **PIG**

10 February 1948 – 27 January 1960

1948	10 February	1948 – 28 January	1949 **RAT**
1949	29 January	1949 – 16 February	1950 **OX**
1950	17 February	1950 – 5 February	1951 **TIGER**
1951	6 February	1951 – 26 January	1952 **RABBIT**
1952	27 January	1952 – 13 February	1953 **DRAGON**
1953	14 February	1953 – 2 February	1954 **SNAKE**
1954	3 February	1954 – 23 January	1955 **HORSE**
1955	24 January	1955 – 11 February	1956 **GOAT**
1956	12 February	1956 – 30 January	1957 **MONKEY**
1957	31 January	1957 – 17 February	1958 **ROOSTER**
1958	18 February	1958 – 7 February	1959 **DOG**
1959	8 February	1959 – 27 January	1960 **PIG**

28 January 1960 – 14 February 1972

1960	28 January	1960 – 14 February 1961	**RAT**
1961	15 February	1961 – 4 February 1962	**OX**
1962	5 February	1962 – 24 January 1963	**TIGER**
1963	25 January	1963 – 12 February 1964	**RABBIT**
1964	13 February	1964 – 1 February 1965	**DRAGON**
1965	2 February	1965 – 20 January 1966	**SNAKE**
1966	21 January	1966 – 8 February 1967	**HORSE**
1967	9 February	1967 – 29 January 1968	**GOAT**
1968	30 January	1968 – 16 February 1969	**MONKEY**
1969	17 February	1969 – 5 February 1970	**ROOSTER**
1970	6 February	1970 – 26 January 1971	**DOG**
1971	27 January	1971 – 14 February 1972	**PIG**

15 February 1972 – 1 February 1984

1972	15 February	1972 – 2 February 1973	**RAT**
1973	3 February	1973 – 22 January 1974	**OX**
1974	23 January	1974 – 10 February 1975	**TIGER**
1975	11 February	1975 – 30 January 1976	**RABBIT**
1976	31 January	1976 – 17 February 1977	**DRAGON**
1977	18 February	1977 – 6 February 1978	**SNAKE**
1978	7 February	1978 – 27 January 1979	**HORSE**
1979	28 January	1979 – 15 February 1980	**GOAT**
1980	16 February	1980 – 4 February 1981	**MONKEY**
1981	5 February	1981 – 24 January 1982	**ROOSTER**
1982	25 January	1982 – 12 February 1983	**DOG**
1983	13 February	1983 – 1 February 1984	**PIG**

2 February 1984 – 18 February 1996

1984	2 February 1984 – 19 February 1985	**RAT**
1985	20 February 1985 – 8 February 1986	**OX**
1986	9 February 1986 – 28 January 1987	**TIGER**
1987	29 January 1987 – 16 February 1988	**RABBIT**
1988	17 February 1988 – 5 February 1989	**DRAGON**
1989	6 February 1989 – 26 January 1990	**SNAKE**
1990	27 January 1990 – 14 February 1991	**HORSE**
1991	15 February 1991 – 3 February 1992	**GOAT**
1992	4 February 1992 – 22 January 1993	**MONKEY**
1993	23 January 1993 – 9 February 1994	**ROOSTER**
1994	10 February 1994 – 30 January 1995	**DOG**
1995	31 January 1995 – 18 February 1996	**PIG**

19 February 1996 – 6 February 2008

1996	19 February 1996 – 7 February 1997	**RAT**
1997	8 February 1997 – 27 January 1998	**OX**
1998	28 January 1998 – 5 February 1999	**TIGER**
1999	6 February 1999 – 4 February 2000	**RABBIT**
2000	5 February 2000 – 23 January 2001	**DRAGON**
2001	24 January 2001 – 11 February 2002	**SNAKE**
2002	12 February 2002 – 31 January 2003	**HORSE**
2003	1 February 2003 – 21 January 2004	**GOAT**
2004	22 January 2004 – 8 February 2005	**MONKEY**
2005	9 February 2005 – 28 January 2006	**ROOSTER**
2006	29 January 2006 – 17 February 2007	**DOG**
2007	18 February 2007 – 6 February 2008	**PIG**

The Rat
The Yang water animal

The rat was welcomed in ancient times as a protector and a bringer of material prosperity.

THE RAT PERSONALITY

Anxious not to be a failure, the affable, elegant and generous rat lives for today. When rat is being a charming socialite or a light-hearted gossip, this animal should never be underestimated. Attracted to whatever is clandestine, secretive or a potential bargain, the rat is a very clever animal who enjoys taking the best possible advantage of all situations.

Lunar years ruled by the rat

1900 – 1901
31 January – 18 February

1912 – 1913
18 February – 5 February

1924 – 1925
5 February – 24 January

1936 – 1937
24 January – 10 February

1948 – 1949
10 February – 28 January

1960 – 1961
28 January – 14 February

1972 – 1973
15 February – 2 February

1984 – 1985
2 February – 19 February

1996 – 1997
19 February – 7 February

RAT ASSOCIATIONS
PLANTS AND FLOWERS
  SAVORY, WORMWOOD, ORCHID, THISLE
FOOD AND TASTE
  PEAS, PORK, SALT
SEASONS AND TIMES
  WINTER, COLD
BIRTH
  ANYTIME IN THE SUMMER
COLOURS
  WHITE, BLACK, BLUE

© DIAGRAM

Secret rat

Some rats suffer from a morbid guilt. Almost all fear failure so are often in a rat race. The rat's calm exterior hides inner aggressive restlessness. Rats tend to be gullible, falling into rat-traps, but they learn from experience so are constantly on guard.

Element

Rat is linked to the ancient Chinese element of water. Water endows rat with qualities of quiet restraint, persistence, diplomacy and the ability to predict future trends, especially in business and the material world. Water rats can influence others but need to turn their inner restlessness into active leadership.

TEN GOOD RAT QUALITIES

1. AFFECTIONATE
2. CHARMING
3. CONSTRUCTIVE CRITIC
4. HONEST
5. IMAGINATIVE
6. INTELLIGENT
7. OPPORTUNISTIC
8. PASSIONATE
9. PRACTICAL
10. QUICKLY LEARNS FROM EXPERIENCE

TEN RAT LIKES

1. COMPANY
2. BEING THE FIRST TO EXPLORE NEW PLACES
3. ENTERTAINING
4. GOOD-QUALITY WORLDLY POSSESSIONS
5. MONEY
6. MYSTERIES
7. ODDITIES/THE UNUSUAL
8. TAKING A GAMBLE
9. FINDING SOLUTIONS
10. PLEASURE

Balance

The rat itself is Yang, but it is associated with the element water which is Yin, so rat people have a built-in potential for good balance. The Yin tendency of water, linked with night, darkness and introversion, can make good use of the resources of Yang, which is linked with day, light and extrovert initiative. For example, Yin has a natural inclination to respond to opportunities as they occur. Therefore, to thrive, rats have to work hard in response to situations not immediately under their control. This is stressful for rats, but their innate Yang tendency enables rats also to create opportunities for themselves, thus removing the stress and keeping labours to a minimum. Rats do not enjoy very hard work, especially that which is thrust upon them.

TEN BAD RAT QUALITIES
1. CALCULATING
2. A BUSYBODY
3. A GRUMBLER
4. MEAN
5. A GOSSIP AND A SCANDALMONGER
6. AN OBSESSIVE HOARDER
7. OVERAMBITIOUS
8. QUICK-TEMPERED
9. RESTLESS
10. HAS ULTERIOR MOTIVES

TEN RAT DISLIKES
1. AGENDAS
2. ALARM CLOCKS
3. ANY KIND OF FAILURE
4. BEING ISOLATED
5. BUREAUCRACY
6. HAVING NOTHING TO DO
7. RED TAPE
8. MUNDANE EVERYDAY LIFE
9. RIGID TIMETABLES
10. MANUAL LABOUR

The Ox
The Yin water animal

In China, many people do not eat beef as the ox is respected for the help it gives in working the land. The ox is associated with water and figures of oxen were once thrown into rivers to prevent flooding.

Lunar years ruled by the ox

1901 – 1902
19 February – 7 February

1913 – 1914
6 February – 25 January

1925 – 1926
25 January – 12 February

1937 – 1938
11 February – 30 January

1949 – 1950
29 January – 16 February

1961 – 1962
15 February – 4 February

1973 – 1974
3 February – 22 January

1985 – 1986
20 February – 8 February

1997 – 1998
8 February – 27 January

THE OX PERSONALITY

Basically, oxen are honest, straightforward, kind-hearted people – often described as down-to-earth. Oxen have great reserves of strength to call on and are very hard-working. They are normally easy to get on with because they have no duplicity in them. Oxen do exactly what they say, and mean what they say. Despite being respectable and conventional, oxen are very independent-minded and not easily swayed by the opinions of others. They cannot take advice very well and can be intolerant and scathing to those they disagree with.

OX ASSOCIATIONS
PLANTS AND FLOWERS
  HEMP, ORCHID
FOOD AND TASTE
  GINGER, SWEET
SEASONS AND TIMES
  WINTER, COLD, WET
BIRTH
  SUMMER NIGHT
COLOURS
  YELLOW, BLUE

TEN GOOD OX QUALITIES

1. CAPABLE
2. CLEAR-THINKING
3. CONSCIENTIOUS
4. DETERMINED
5. GENTLE
6. HARD-WORKING
7. PATIENT
8. PRACTICAL
9. RELIABLE
10. STRONG

Secret ox

The image of the ox is that of a placid person. Mostly this is true. If, however, oxen are provoked or their patience stretched too far they can act like bulls shown a red rag. This hot-tempered side of ox's nature is well hidden but always present. Also, despite their homely images oxen are actually very innovative and creative people.

Element

Ox is linked to the ancient Chinese element of water. Water is linked to the arts and expressiveness. In oxen, however, water is more likely to be stagnant, and passively, rather than actively, expressed. Bear in mind, water can be both as nurturing as rain or as destructive as a hurricane.

TEN OX LIKES

1. HAND-MADE CRAFTS
2. HOME-COOKED FOOD
3. SENSIBLE CLOTHES
4. SOBER OR EARTHY COLOURS
5. THE FAMILIAR
6. TO BE APPRECIATED
7. TO PLAN AHEAD
8. TO SAVE MONEY
9. TRADITIONAL FESTIVALS LIKE SHROVE TUESDAY
10. GARDENING

Balance

Oxen value their privacy highly. They very rarely confide their feelings to anyone. Oxen go to great lengths to keep their innermost secrets and the barriers they build to protect themselves can become a prison. Unless people born in the year of the ox learn to balance this need for privacy with a more open and relaxed attitude to their emotions, they will become neurotic and suffer from self-delusion, as too much repression can direct the ox's quite formidable energies inward.

TEN BAD OX QUALITIES

1. BIASED
2. COMPLACENT
3. CONSERVATIVE
4. DOGMATIC
5. DULL
6. GLOOMY
7. HOT-TEMPERED
8. INTOLERANT
9. MATERIALISTIC
10. STUBBORN

TEN OX DISLIKES

1. FADS AND FASHIONS
2. FOOLISHNESS
3. GARISH COLOURS
4. HEART-TO-HEART CHATS
5. MODERN ART
6. NOVELTIES/GIMMICKS
7. STRESSFUL JOBS
8. BEING TAKEN FOR GRANTED
9. INVOLUNTARY CHANGE
10. WASHING DIRTY LINEN IN PUBLIC

The Tiger
The Yang wood animal

Associated with good fortune, power and royalty, tigers are viewed with both fear and respect. Their protection and wisdom is sought after. The Chinese see the tiger, and not the lion, as the king of animals.

THE TIGER PERSONALITY

Tigers are contrary creatures. The striped coat reflects tiger's ambivalent nature. Tigers are creatures of great strength and ability; but how this is used can vary greatly. They are born leaders or rebels, and instinctively protective, though prone to taking risks, so it may not always be wise to follow one. Often critical, tigers make fine revolutionaries. Once involved in battle, they usually come out on top, though their impetuosity can be their downfall.

Lunar years ruled by the tiger

1902 – 1903
8 February – 28 January

1914 – 1915
26 January – 13 February

1926 – 1927
13 February – 1 February

1938 – 1939
31 January – 18 February

1950 – 1951
17 February – 5 February

1962 – 1963
5 February – 24 January

1974 – 1975
23 January – 10 February

1986 – 1987
9 February – 28 January

1998 – 1999
28 January – 5 February

TIGER ASSOCIATIONS
PLANTS AND FLOWERS
  BAMBOO, HELIOTROPE
FOOD AND TASTE
  BREAD, POULTRY, ACID
SEASONS AND TIMES
  WINTER, SPRING, WINDY
BIRTH
  NIGHT
COLOURS
  ORANGE, DARK GOLD

TEN GOOD TIGER QUALITIES

1. BENEVOLENT
2. COURAGEOUS
3. DARING
4. DETERMINED
5. GENEROUS
6. HONOURABLE
7. LOYAL
8. PROTECTIVE
9. SENSITIVE
10. WISE

Secret tiger

On the surface, tigers may appear peaceful and controlled. Hidden underneath, however, there is often an aggressive and even belligerent nature. Also, surprisingly, when faced with difficult decisions, the seemingly decisive tiger has a tendency to retreat into procrastination.

Element

Tiger is linked to the ancient Chinese element of wood. The symbolism of wood is as ambivalent as that of the tiger. As a tree, wood's branches reach for the sky while its roots anchor it in the earth. This endows tiger with the ability (not necessarily used) to moderate his impulsive behaviour. Yet wood also gives the tiger passion, which can either lend gentleness to their behaviour or it may make them violent and destructive.

TEN TIGER LIKES

1. A CHALLENGE
2. ANYTHING NEW OR UNUSUAL
3. BEING IN CHARGE
4. BIG PARTIES
5. FLATTERY
6. HONESTY IN OTHERS AND THEMSELVES
7. SPENDING MONEY
8. SUCCESS
9. SURPRISES
10. TO BE THEIR OWN PERSON

Balance

The tiger itself is Yang; its striped coat, however, represents the union of both Yin and Yang forces – the balance of which confers great power. It is this contradiction that is at the heart of understanding the nature of tigers. So, while tigers have huge potential, it is a potential for both success or failure. Although usually fortunate, tigers are predisposed to dangerous situations. If they act wisely, tigers can take advantage of this and become very successful. Otherwise, they may fail on a grand scale. Whether a tiger is calm and wise or impetuous and hot-headed in the use of power depends on the individual's ability to learn from experience, heed advice and channel their energy constructively.

TEN BAD TIGER QUALITIES
1. AGGRESSIVE
2. ARROGANT
3. CRITICAL
4. DEMANDING
5. DISOBEDIENT
6. IMPATIENT
7. QUARRELSOME
8. SELFISH
9. STUBBORN
10. VAIN

TEN TIGER DISLIKES
1. BEING IGNORED
2. FAILURE
3. FEELING CAGED IN BY CIRCUMSTANCES/PEOPLE
4. HYPOCRISY
5. JEWELS AND TRINKETS
6. NURSING OTHERS
7. PAYING ATTENTION TO DETAIL
8. SCANDALMONGERING
9. RULES AND LAWS MADE BY OTHERS
10. TAKING ORDERS

The Rabbit
The Yin wood animal

The rabbit is associated with longevity and the moon. Some astrologers identify this sign as the cat, not rabbit, but Chinese astrologers always refer to it as the rabbit or hare.

Lunar years ruled by the rabbit

1903 – 1904
29 January – 15 February

1915 – 1916
14 February – 2 February

1927 – 1928
2 February – 22 January

1939 – 1940
19 February – 7 February

1951 – 1952
6 February – 26 January

1963 – 1964
25 January – 12 February

1975 – 1976
11 February – 30 January

1987 – 1988
29 January – 16 February

1999 – 2000
6 February – 4 February

THE RABBIT PERSONALITY

Seemingly unexceptional, rabbits provoke extreme reactions. They inspire either adoration or hate, but never indifference. Rabbits are mysterious yet practical, timid but ruthless, articulate but inscrutable, and virtuous as well as cunning. They like their lives to be secure, comfortable and calm, yet they are fiercely independent. Sensitive and intuitive by nature, rabbits are easily influenced by their emotions.

RABBIT ASSOCIATIONS
PLANTS AND FLOWERS
  FIG TREE, QUEEN ANNE'S LACE
FOOD AND TASTE
  WHEAT, POULTRY, ACID
SEASONS AND TIMES
  SPRING, WINDY
BIRTH
  SUMMER
COLOUR
  WHITE

Secret rabbit

Mistakenly, people often assume that rabbits' need for security and comfort combined with the urge to avoid confrontation means that they are weak. This is not true. Rabbits will use all their diplomacy, charm and cunning to achieve their ends. The fact that they very rarely need to resort to outright battle to get their own way is proof of rabbits' strength, not weakness, of character.

TEN GOOD RABBIT QUALITIES
1. DIPLOMATIC
2. HONOURABLE
3. HOSPITABLE
4. INTELLIGENT
5. INTUITIVE
6. PEACEFUL
7. REFINED
8. REFLECTIVE
9. SENSITIVE
10. WELL-ORGANIZED

TEN RABBIT LIKES
1. BEAUTIFUL PAINTINGS
2. COMFORTABLE HOME
3. LONG HAIRSTYLES
4. ATTENTION TO DETAIL
5. CONVERSATION/GOSSIP
6. PRIVACY
7. ROMANTIC FILMS
8. SECRETS/MYSTERIES
9. TO USE THEIR WITS TO SOLVE A PROBLEM
10. TO HAVE A ROUTINE

Element

Rabbit is linked to the ancient Chinese element of wood. Wood can be both flexible like a sapling or sturdy as an oak. How its energy is expressed depends on how well a wood person can both control and indulge their natural tendencies. For a rabbit, the tendencies to be watched are the urge to avoid change or trouble at all costs, self-indulgence and timidity.

TEN BAD RABBIT QUALITIES

1. CONFORMIST
2. HESITANT
3. CUNNING
4. EGOTISTICAL
5. FAINT-HEARTED
6. GOSSIPY
7. INDECISIVE
8. SECRETIVE
9. SUPERFICIAL
10. UNPREDICTABLE

Balance

The behaviour of a rabbit can be unpredictable as it varies according to current circumstances. During peaceful times, rabbits will be at ease and relaxed. Sudden changes, unforeseen events or conflicts will unbalance rabbits and make them irritable, confused, and even aggressive. Rabbit people will not be happy at such times until they are back in control of the situation. Also, rabbit personalities need to balance their self-preoccupied Yin natures and occasionally try to see things from another's point of view.

TEN RABBIT DISLIKES

1. ARGUMENTS
2. COMMITMENTS
3. COMPLICATED PLANS
4. DRASTIC CHANGE
5. SURPRISES
6. TAKING RISKS
7. TO WITNESS SUFFERING
8. TO CHANGE THEIR MIND
9. TO SAY ANYTHING UNPLEASANT
10. TO SEE/USE VIOLENCE

The Dragon
The Yang wood animal

The dragon is the only mythical animal in the Chinese zodiac. In China, dragons are associated with strength, health, harmony and good luck; they are placed above doors or on the tops of roofs to banish demons and evil spirits.

Lunar years ruled by the dragon

1904 – 1905
16 February – 3 February

1916 – 1917
3 February – 22 January

1928 – 1929
23 January – 9 February

1940 – 1941
8 February – 26 January

1952 – 1953
27 January – 13 February

1964 – 1965
13 February – 1 February

1976 – 1977
31 January – 17 February

1988 – 1989
17 February – 5 February

2000 – 2001
5 February – 23 January

THE DRAGON PERSONALITY

Dragons have magnetic, persuasive personalities and are capable of great success or spectacular failure. Normally, however, whatever they set their hearts on doing, they do well; the secret is their great faith in themselves. On the negative side, dragons are renowned for not finishing what they start. The frank and open way in which they approach people and situations can be disconcerting; but their innate sincerity and enthusiasm make up for this.

DRAGON ASSOCIATIONS
PLANTS AND FLOWERS
MANDRAKE, SAGE, LOTUS
FOOD AND TASTE
WHEAT, POULTRY, ACID
SEASONS AND TIMES
SPRING, WINDY
BIRTH
ANYTIME, EXCEPT
DURING A STORM
COLOURS
YELLOW, BLACK

Secret dragon

Despite their impressive appearance, deep down dragons are dissatisfied and discontent. The dragon's tireless search for excitement is not always fruitful. They need to be embarking on some new project, campaign or love affair to feel truly alive. Inevitably, depression caused by the unavoidable daily routine will get most dragons down at some time.

TEN GOOD DRAGON QUALITIES
1. DYNAMIC
2. ENTHUSIASTIC
3. EXCITING
4. IDEALISTIC
5. INTELLIGENT
6. IRRESISTIBLE
7. LUCKY
8. SENTIMENTAL
9. SUCCESSFUL
10. VISIONARY

TEN DRAGON LIKES
1. BEING ASKED FOR HELP
2. CELEBRATIONS, PARTIES & FESTIVALS
3. CHAMPIONING CAUSES
4. FUN FAIRS, ESPECIALLY THE ROLLER COASTER
5. GIVING ADVICE
6. GOING ON HOLIDAY AND TRAVELLING
7. JAZZ MUSIC
8. PICNICS
9. TO BE IN CHARGE
10. TO FEEL IRREPLACEABLE

Element

Dragon is linked to the ancient Chinese element of wood. Wood is an ambivalent element. As a crutch it lends support; as a spear it can be used as a weapon. Consequently, dragons are full of both positive and negative energies that will surface in, for example, strong emotions. For instance, emotionally, wood is associated with both anger and kindness. Wood is also responsible for growth and renewal, so dragons tend to be creative people.

TEN BAD DRAGON QUALITIES

1. DEMANDING
2. DISSATISFIED
3. GULLIBLE
4. IMPATIENT
5. INTOLERANT
6. IRRITABLE
7. OVERPOWERING
8. OVERZEALOUS
9. SHORT-TEMPERED
10. TACTLESS

TEN DRAGON DISLIKES

1. BEING PATRONIZED
2. A LACK OF ENERGY OR WILLPOWER IN OTHERS
3. COMPROMISE
4. A LACK OF VISION IN OTHERS
5. DISHONESTY/HYPOCRISY
6. HAVING NOTHING TO DO
7. HAVING TO BE PATIENT
8. LISTENING TO ADVICE
9. WAITING FOR ANYTHING
10. MANIPULATIVE PEOPLE

Balance

Dragons spend a lot of time racing from one experience to another. Always set on the latest goal, they are blinkered to failure and try to forget any that occur. Only successes are considered significant. Dragons seem impressive only because they believe that they are, and this amazing self-confidence makes others believe in them also. You could say that the dragon's image is simply a confidence trick. According to Chinese tradition, dragons must confront their image and recognize its illusory nature. Dragons will only be truly content when they accept their vulnerability, and use it to balance their exuberance.

The Snake
The Yin fire animal

There are few animals with more symbolic associations than the snake. Chinese mythology holds that a half-human snake was the father of the Chinese emperors.

THE SNAKE PERSONALITY

In the West, the snake is often seen as evil. The snake of Chinese astrology, however, is associated with beauty and wisdom. Snakes may appear languid and serene, but they are always mentally active. Snakes are deep thinkers and give very good advice – but they cannot take it. Snakes are capable of lying to get out of a scrape. Linked with esoteric knowledge and spiritual discovery, snakes are sacred to many peoples. Snakes are often people who are, or are interested in, the psychic, the mystical or the religious.

Lunar years ruled by the snake

1905 – 1906
4 February – 24 January

1917 – 1918
23 January – 10 February

1929 – 1930
10 February – 29 January

1941 – 1942
27 January – 14 February

1953 – 1954
14 February – 2 February

1965 – 1966
2 February – 20 January

1977 – 1978
18 February – 6 February

1989 – 1990
6 February – 26 January

2001 – 2002
24 January – 11 February

SNAKE ASSOCIATIONS
PLANTS AND FLOWERS
  FERNS, HEATHER, THISTLE
FOOD AND TASTE
  RICE, LAMB, BITTER
SEASONS AND TIMES
  SUMMER, HOT, SUNNY
BIRTH
  WARM SUMMER DAY
COLOURS
  GREEN, RED

TEN GOOD SNAKE QUALITIES

1. CURIOUS
2. DISTINGUISHED
3. ORGANIZED
4. PERCEPTIVE
5. REFLECTIVE
6. SELF-CONTAINED
7. SENSUAL
8. SHREWD
9. SOPHISTICATED
10. WISE

Secret snake

The typical image of a snake is one basking in the sun doing nothing. Many interpret this as laziness. In fact, snakes are very hard-working. If something needs to be done, snake will not shy away from it. The secret is their efficiency. Snakes will get the job done in the quickest, most economical way, which is why they always have plenty of time to relax.

Element

Snake is linked to the ancient Chinese element of fire. Fire is a dynamic, exciting sign, which is balanced by snake's innate Yin tendency. The energy of fire can be expressed positively and negatively. It brings warmth, comfort and light, and it protects. But fire can also burn and destroy. For example, emotionally fire is associated with cruelty and intolerance as well as love and respect. Fire people are always attractive.

TEN SNAKE LIKES

1. A GOOD DEBATE
2. ABSTRACT ART
3. APPLAUSE
4. DESERTS AND WILD LANDSCAPES
5. DRESSING TO IMPRESS
6. HARMONY AND STABILITY
7. ORNAMENTS
8. TO BE ASKED FOR HELP
9. TO IMPRESS OTHERS
10. TO PLEASE OTHERS

Balance

Snakes and dragons are especially karmic signs. Put simply, karma is a person's destiny. Each action performed affects the next and so on, into infinity. The Chinese believe that snakes particularly must deal with their karmic problems within their lifetime to achieve balance. This should not be too much of a problem as snakes are generally well-balanced people. Their natural wisdom grants them the ability to deal with life gracefully and they are usually unperturbed by life's ups and downs.

TEN BAD SNAKE QUALITIES
1. ANXIOUS
2. CALCULATING
3. CRUEL
4. DISHONEST
5. EXTRAVAGANT
6. JEALOUS
7. OBSTINATE
8. POSSESSIVE
9. SELF-DOUBTING
10. VENGEFUL

TEN SNAKE DISLIKES
1. DISPUTES AND VIOLENCE
2. ANYTHING FAKE
3. PEOPLE GETTING OUT OF CONTROL
4. PREJUDICED PEOPLE
5. SUPERFICIAL PEOPLE
6. TO BE ABANDONED
7. TO BE MADE AN EXAMPLE OF
8. TO BE FOUND GULLIBLE
9. TO LEND OTHERS MONEY
10. VULGARITY

Tendencies to watch are their highly individual approach to morality and honesty – that is, snakes do or say whatever is most convenient for them.

The Horse
The Yang fire animal

The horse is associated with grace, elegance, bravery and nobility. In China, the horse is the symbol of freedom.

THE HORSE PERSONALITY

Horses approach life with contagious enthusiasm. They are usually happy and will have many friends. They love to chat, converse or orate. Horses have good images – others see in their zest for life bravery and independence – but they are actually quite cowardly. Although they love freedom, horses are not truly independent as they rely on others for support and encouragement that is vital to their wellbeing.

Lunar years ruled by the horse

1906 – 1907
25 January – 12 February

1918 – 1919
11 February – 31 January

1930 – 1931
30 January – 16 February

1942 – 1943
15 February – 4 February

1954 – 1955
3 February – 23 January

1966 – 1967
21 January – 8 February

1978 – 1979
7 February – 27 January

1990 – 1991
27 January – 14 February

2002 – 2003
12 February – 31 January

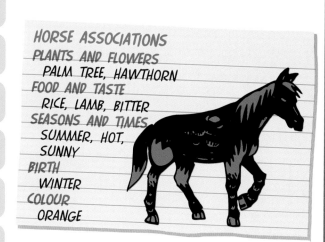

HORSE ASSOCIATIONS
PLANTS AND FLOWERS
   PALM TREE, HAWTHORN
FOOD AND TASTE
   RICE, LAMB, BITTER
SEASONS AND TIMES
   SUMMER, HOT,
   SUNNY
BIRTH
   WINTER
COLOUR
   ORANGE

© DIAGRAM

Secret horse

On the surface, horses appear to be very self-assured and fearless. Underneath, however, horses are weak and fragile creatures. They are easily scared and let themselves get carried away by their emotions.

Element

Horse is linked to the ancient Chinese element of fire. Fire is a dynamic, exciting sign, which is enhanced by the horse's innate Yang tendency. The energy of fire can be expressed both positively and negatively. It brings warmth, light and protection as well as the ability to burn and destroy. In horses, fire expresses itself erratically, making them both dynamic and temperamental.

TEN GOOD HORSE QUALITIES

1. CHEERFUL
2. ENTERPRISING
3. ENTHUSIASTIC
4. FLEXIBLE
5. GENEROUS
6. LOYAL
7. NOBLE
8. SINCERE
9. UNSELFISH
10. VERSATILE

TEN HORSE LIKES

1. A CHANGE OF SCENERY
2. BEGINNING PROJECTS
3. CHAT AND GOSSIP
4. DANCING
5. EXPENSIVE RESTAURANTS
6. GOING ON A VOYAGE
7. MEETING NEW PEOPLE
8. TO BE COMPLIMENTED
9. TO DISCUSS EMOTIONS
10. TO FEEL PIONEERING

Balance

Horses are both fire and Yang. Therefore, they naturally have great reserves of strength. Yet people born under this sign, although seemingly self-confident, are too easily affected by the opinions of others. Criticism or hostility, no matter how slight, shatters their vulnerable egos. Horses will only have access to their full strengths when they have learned to balance their need for approval with faith in themselves.

TEN BAD HORSE QUALITIES
1. ANXIOUS
2. CARELESS
3. EASILY PANICKED
4. IMPATIENT
5. INSECURE
6. IRRESPONSIBLE
7. SPENDTHRIFT
8. SUPERFICIAL
9. TEMPERAMENTAL
10. VAIN

TEN HORSE DISLIKES
1. BEING BORED
2. BEING TOLD WHAT TO DO
3. BUREAUCRATS
4. CRITICISM/COMPLAINTS
5. DISAPPROVAL
6. LISTENING TO OTHERS
7. SCHEDULES/TIMETABLES
8. SOLITUDE
9. UNCOMMUNICATIVE PEOPLE
10. DISINTERESTED PEOPLE

The Goat
The Yin fire animal

The goat is associated with harmony, creativity, peace and pleasure. In China, the goat is seen as a harbinger of peace.

THE GOAT PERSONALITY
Charming, amiable and sympathetic, goats are genuinely nice people. They hate to criticize and always look for the best in people – including themselves. A goat will prefer to forget grievances rather than brood over them and will bottle up resentments to keep the peace. Goat people live in the present, which they enjoy to the best of their abilities. Thanks to their sensitive natures, goats are one of the most artistic and creative of all the Chinese horoscope signs.

Lunar years ruled by the goat

1907 – 1908
13 February – 1 February

1919 – 1920
1 February – 19 February

1931 – 1932
17 February – 5 February

1943 – 1944
5 February – 24 January

1955 – 1956
24 January – 11 February

1967 – 1968
9 February – 29 January

1979 – 1980
28 January – 15 February

1991 – 1992
15 February – 3 February

2003 – 2004
1 February – 21 January

GOAT ASSOCIATIONS
PLANTS AND FLOWERS
  WORMWOOD, ANISE,
  HONEYSUCKLE
FOOD AND TASTE
  RICE, LAMB, BITTER
SEASONS AND TIMES
  SUMMER, HOT
BIRTH
  RAINY DAY
COLOUR
  SKY-BLUE

TEN GOOD GOAT QUALITIES

1. ADAPTABLE
2. CREATIVE
3. EASY-GOING
4. FAITHFUL
5. HONEST
6. IMAGINATIVE
7. INDEPENDENT
8. INGENIOUS
9. PEACEFUL
10. SINCERE

Secret goat

From their description, people may think that goats are weak creatures who are easy to take advantage of. In reality, however, they will fight violently if something important to them is threatened. Fortunately, as goats apportion value according to very personal criteria, what they would defend to the last is not often something that others covet.

Element

Goat is linked to the ancient Chinese element of fire. Fire is a dynamic, exciting and energetic sign. In the case of goats, fire expresses itself in their imaginative and creative abilities. Normally, fire people are as fiery as the sign suggests. The easy-going and carefree nature of the goat, however, dampens their fiery sides, which are kept well hidden until times of crisis.

TEN GOAT LIKES

1. BEAUTIFUL PEOPLE
2. BEAUTY
3. COSTUME DRAMAS
4. MARBLE STATUES
5. PARKS WITH FOUNTAINS
6. TO BE TAKEN CARE OF
7. TO FORGIVE AND FORGET
8. TO PLEASE OTHERS
9. TO MAKE PEOPLE CURIOUS
10. TRANQUILLITY

Balance

Normally, people are advised to look to themselves to balance the strengths and weaknesses of their characters. For example, the goat would be advised to try and take more care of the practical side of life – such as paying the bills – and not rely on others to support them as they pursue their own interests. Chinese tradition, however, holds that goats are mostly unable to change this aspect of their natures. Therefore, they will need to find a patron to take care of the 'administration' of their life and allow them the freedom to make the most of their creative talents. This role could be filled by, for example, a devoted husband or wife, a manager or even a loyal accountant!

TEN BAD GOAT QUALITIES
1. ANXIOUS
2. CARELESS
3. DISORGANIZED
4. GULLIBLE
5. IMPRACTICAL
6. IMPULSIVE
7. INDULGENT
8. IRRATIONAL
9. IRRESPONSIBLE
10. LAZY

TEN GOAT DISLIKES
1. DOING THE ACCOUNTS
2. EMOTIONAL SCENES
3. HOSTILE ATMOSPHERES
4. OBLIGATIONS
5. ROUTINES
6. TAKING THE INITIATIVE
7. TO BE INVOLVED IN OTHERS' PROBLEMS
8. TO BE MADE TO CHOOSE
9. UNWANTED RESPONSIBILITY
10. TO OFFEND OTHERS

The Monkey
The Yang metal animal

In some parts of China, the monkey is worshipped as the 'Great Sage Equal to Heaven'. Monkeys are also associated with adultery, justice and, emotionally, with sorrow.

Lunar years ruled by the monkey

1908 – 1909
2 February – 21 January

1920 – 1921
20 February – 7 February

1932 – 1933
6 February – 25 January

1944 – 1945
25 January – 12 February

1956 – 1957
12 February – 30 January

1968 – 1969
30 January – 16 February

1980 – 1981
16 February – 4 February

1992 – 1993
4 February – 22 January

2004 – 2005
22 January – 8 February

THE MONKEY PERSONALITY

Highly competitive and insatiably curious, monkeys are very shrewd. They are intelligent and ingenious and try to make the best of any situation. Monkeys are quick-witted and never at a loss for words. They have a reputation for trickery. Although monkeys can be scheming and are good at manipulating people, they use these skills wisely. Despite this, monkeys are quick to stop others manipulating them. Monkeys try to be honest but will tell a lie if it is convenient.

MONKEY ASSOCIATIONS
PLANTS AND FLOWERS
    CHINESE WOLFBERRY,
    BIRD OF PARADISE
FOOD AND TASTE
    CLOVES, PUNGENT
SEASONS AND TIMES
    AUTUMN, DRY
BIRTH
    SUMMER
COLOURS
    WHITE

Secret monkey

In public, monkeys always appear light-hearted and carefree. In private, however, they may be nursing deep feelings of insecurity. Monkeys get very hurt if they feel rejected or shut out – but they will make light of the situation and cover their true feelings.

TEN GOOD MONKEY QUALITIES
1. ENTHUSIASTIC
2. ENTERTAINING
3. GENEROUS
4. INVENTIVE
5. LIVELY
6. OPTIMISTIC
7. QUICK-WITTED
8. SOCIABLE
9. TOLERANT
10. VIVACIOUS

TEN MONKEY LIKES
1. A CHALLENGE
2. CASTING HOROSCOPES
3. DECORATING THEIR HOUSE
4. ETHNIC ART
5. NIGHT CLUBS
6. PRACTICAL JOKES
7. TO CARE FOR PEOPLE
8. TO TRAVEL
9. LISTENING TO OTHER'S PROBLEMS/WORRIES
10. VISITING FRIENDS

Element

Monkey is linked to the ancient Chinese element of metal. This is a very strong element. It can be seen positively as a valuable resource, such as gold; or negatively as a weapon, such as a sword. In monkeys, the energy of metal expresses itself as their imaginative, ambitious and independent streaks.

TEN BAD MONKEY QUALITIES

1. CUNNING
2. DISHONEST
3. FICKLE
4. MANIPULATIVE
5. MISCHIEVOUS
6. OPINIONATED
7. SCHEMING
8. SECRETIVE
9. SELFISH
10. VAIN

Balance

Monkeys are curious people, who find something of interest anywhere. They are attracted to the new and unknown. This can make them broad-minded and knowledgeable people, but their energies can be dissipated by these many interests. Monkeys need to learn how to channel their energies into one particular goal at a time. If they can balance their need to search for fresh pastures by bringing some routine or stability into their life, they will find that they can achieve considerable success.

TEN MONKEY DISLIKES

1. BEING MANIPULATED
2. COMPROMISING THEIR INDEPENDENCE
3. CONVENTIONAL PEOPLE
4. DEPENDING ON OTHERS
5. DOING WITHOUT MONEY
6. ESTABLISHED RELIGIONS
7. PUBS AND ALCOHOL
8. PHYSICAL WORK
9. ROUTINE
10. THE ACHIEVEMENTS OF OTHERS

The Rooster
The Yin metal animal

In China, the rooster is associated with the five virtues: fortune, courage, goodness, confidence and military honour.

THE ROOSTER PERSONALITY

Roosters are flamboyant people. Appearance is very important to them and roosters are constantly improving themselves as they are never satisfied with how they look. Roosters are also friendly, pleasant and obliging people. At times of crisis, they prove themselves to be resourceful and talented. Roosters have the wisdom to take life as it comes and keep their attitudes relaxed. They are genuinely independent and rely on none but themselves for moral support and for solutions to their problems.

Lunar years ruled by the rooster

1909 – 1910
22 January – 18 February

1921 – 1922
8 February – 27 January

1933 – 1934
26 January – 13 February

1945 – 1946
13 February – 1 February

1957 – 1958
31 January – 17 February

1969 – 1970
17 February – 5 February

1981 – 1982
5 February – 24 January

1993 – 1994
23 January – 9 February

2005 – 2006
9 February – 28 January

ROOSTERS ASSOCIATIONS
PLANTS AND FLOWERS
   ORANGE AND PALM TREES,
   SUNFLOWER
FOOD AND TASTE
   CEREALS, PUNGENT
SEASONS AND TIMES
   AUTUMN, DRY
BIRTH
   SPRING
COLOURS
   YELLOW, WHITE

Secret rooster

For all their bluff and bravado, in reality roosters are very sensitive and vulnerable people. They are susceptible to both flattery and criticism, and so are easily influenced by either. They hide this weakness behind their arrogant facades. Another little-known fact about roosters is that they like to read. They are actually very knowledgeable people but do not display this aspect of themselves. A rooster would rather be judged on appearance than intelligence.

TEN GOOD ROOSTER QUALITIES
1. CHARITABLE
2. COURAGEOUS
3. ENTERTAINING
4. ENTHUSIASTIC
5. GENEROUS
6. HONEST
7. LOYAL
8. OBLIGING
9. RESILIENT
10. SINCERE

TEN ROOSTER LIKES
1. FLATTERY
2. PUTTING ON A SHOW
3. RECEIVING ADMIRING LOOKS
4. SEDUCTIONS
5. SERIOUS CONVERSATIONS
6. SPENDING MONEY
7. TIDINESS
8. TO DREAM
9. TO GIVE ADVICE
10. TO MAKE AN ENTRANCE

Element

Rooster is linked to the ancient Chinese element of metal. This is a very strong element. It can be seen positively as a valuable resource, such as gold; or negatively as a weapon, such as a sword. For example, the energy of metal expresses itself supportively and inspirationally as well as destructively and inflexibly. Metal people are also intuitive and ambitious.

Balance

Chinese tradition holds that the lives of roosters will be filled with ups and downs. They will experience both the joys and sorrows that life has to offer; for example, sometimes poor and at other times rich. Roosters should aim to achieve emotional stability. They must balance their larger-than-life images with their vulnerable inner selves. Only then will their lives become calm and productive.

TEN BAD ROOSTER QUALITIES
1. ARGUMENTATIVE
2. ARROGANT
3. BOASTFUL
4. CRITICAL
5. HARSH
6. OSTENTATIOUS
7. PRETENTIOUS
8. THOUGHTLESS
9. VAIN
10. VULNERABLE

TEN ROOSTER DISLIKES
1. BADLY DRESSED PEOPLE
2. INTERFERENCE
3. KEEPING OPINIONS TO THEMSELVES
4. TO LOSE COMPOSURE
5. PRACTICAL JOKES
6. TO BE ASKED DIRECT, PERSONAL QUESTIONS
7. TO CONFIDE IN ANYONE
8. TO DISPLAY THEIR KNOWLEDGE
9. ROUTINE
10. STRESS

The Dog
The Yang metal animal

In China the dog is associated with justice and compassion. Dogs are often described as being the 'champions of the underdogs'.

THE DOG PERSONALITY
Essentially, dogs are honest and noble creatures. They are renowned for being champions of justice and have a tendency to see things in black and white. Dogs are respected for their lively minds and quick tongues, which they use in defence of their chosen cause. Yet dogs are cynics as well as idealists, which produces characters with high moral standards, but they are beset by doubts and anxieties.

Lunar years ruled by the dog

1910 – 1911
10 February – 29 January

1922 – 1923
28 January – 15 February

1934 – 1935
14 February – 3 February

1946 – 1947
2 February – 21 January

1958 – 1959
18 February – 7 February

1970 – 1971
6 February – 26 January

1982 – 1983
25 January – 12 February

1994 – 1995
10 February – 30 January

2006 – 2007
29 January – 17 February

DOG ASSOCIATIONS
PLANTS AND FLOWERS
POPPIES, WATER LILIES, ORANGE BLOSSOMS,
FOOD AND TASTE
OATS, PUNGENT
SEASONS AND TIMES
AUTUMN, DRY
BIRTH
DAYTIME
COLOURS
BLACK, DARK BLUE

TEN GOOD DOG QUALITIES

1. COURAGEOUS
2. DUTIFUL
3. FAITHFUL
4. IMAGINATIVE
5. LOYAL
6. RESPONSIBLE
7. SENSITIVE
8. TOLERANT
9. TRUSTWORTHY
10. WITTY

TEN DOG LIKES

1. DETECTIVE NOVELS
2. ANYTHING ARCANE
3. HORROR MOVIES
4. LEARNING ABOUT OTHER CULTURES
5. NATURAL FABRICS
6. REUNIONS WITH OLD FRIENDS
7. SILVER JEWELLERY
8. TO REMEMBER BIRTHDAYS
9. THINGS OCCULT
10. WRITING LETTERS TO FRIENDS

Secret dog

Despite their courageousness and determination to do good, dogs need to be led. Left on their own, they can become confused and anxious. After all, there are so many deserving causes and not enough time to help everyone. Once they have been given instructions or help, they can move mountains to carry out a task.

Element

Dog is linked to the ancient Chinese element of metal. This is a very strong element. It can be seen positively as a valuable resource, such as gold; or negatively as a weapon, such as a sword. The energy of metal expresses itself in dogs as their strong-minded, idealistic traits. Metal people are usually ambitious; dogs, however, are not personally ambitious. Instead, they are more concerned with the advancement of the downtrodden.

Balance

The main character fault of dogs is their constant worrying and self-doubting natures. A certain amount of stress or anxiety can be useful as it helps motivate the dog, who lacks motivation. But dogs can worry to the extent that it stops them doing anything useful. This interferes with their ability to lead happy and productive lives. Anxious of the future and regretful of the past, dogs need to learn how to live in the present. If they can take each day as it comes, dogs will find that their anxieties lessen. They need to reach a balance between necessary and useful worrying and self-defeating anxiety.

TEN BAD DOG QUALITIES
1. ANXIOUS
2. DISCOURAGING
3. DISTRUSTFUL
4. DOUBTFUL
5. OBSTINATE
6. PESSIMISTIC
7. STRICT
8. SUSPICIOUS
9. TIMID
10. UNADVENTUROUS

TEN DOG DISLIKES
1. DECEIT AND DISHONESTY
2. THE FINANCIAL COST OF AN ACTIVITY
3. FAMILY REUNIONS
4. HYPOCRITES
5. MAN-MADE FABRICS
6. PEDANTS
7. PSYCHOLOGICAL GAMES
8. SELFISH BEHAVIOUR
9. SUPERFICIAL AND AMBITIOUS PEOPLE
10. COCKTAIL PARTIES

The Pig
The Yin water animal

In China, the pig is associated with fertility and virility. To bear children in the year of the pig is considered very fortunate, for they will be happy and honest.

Lunar years ruled by the pig

1911 – 1912
30 January – 17 February

1923 – 1924
16 February – 4 February

1935 – 1936
4 February – 23 January

1947 – 1948
22 January – 9 February

1959 – 1960
8 February – 27 January

1971 – 1972
27 January – 14 February

1983 – 1984
13 February – 1 February

1995 – 1996
31 January – 18 February

2007 – 2008
18 February – 6 February

THE PIG PERSONALITY
Pigs are among the most natural and easy-going personalities around. They are pleasure-loving characters who seek out the good and the fun things in life. Pigs are sympathetic and will always be there for friends at times of trouble. In turn, they look to their friends for advice and support when difficult decisions have to be made. Pigs still like to maintain their independence though and privacy is very important to them.

PIG ASSOCIATIONS
PLANTS AND FLOWERS
  GINSENG, WATER LILY
FOOD AND TASTE
  PEAS, MEAT, SALT
SEASONS AND TIMES
  WINTER, COLD, WET
BIRTH
  WINTER
COLOUR
  BLACK

Secret pig

The western view of pigs attributes to them various negative qualities such as greediness, laziness, filthiness and stupidity. In fact, pigs are none of these things – although they do have a taste for good food. They are not overwhelming characters, but they are careful and determined people who are not easily set back by obstacles.

TEN GOOD PIG QUALITIES
1. CHEERFUL
2. COURTEOUS
3. DETERMINED
4. DILIGENT
5. GENEROUS
6. HONEST
7. PEACEFUL
8. SENSUAL
9. TOLERANT
10. UNCOMPLAINING

TEN PIG LIKES
1. FAMOUS PEOPLE
2. MAKING PRESENTS FOR PEOPLE
3. ORGANIZING PARTIES
4. READING A GOOD BOOK
5. THE SOUND OF APPLAUSE
6. TO BE COMFORTABLE
7. TO BE IN A RELATIONSHIP
8. TO GOSSIP
9. TO WORK AS PART OF A TEAM
10. GOURMET FOOD

Element

Pig is linked to the ancient Chinese element of water. Water is linked to the arts and inner expressiveness. Emotionally, water is associated with fear. It also endows sensitivity and understanding. In pigs, water expresses itself as their nurturing qualities and in their ability to compromise and avoid conflict.

TEN BAD PIG QUALITIES
1. DEBAUCHED
2. DEFENCELESS
3. EXCESSIVE
4. FEARFUL
5. FIERCE-TEMPERED
6. GULLIBLE
7. IMPATIENT
8. INDULGENT
9. MATERIALISTIC
10. SPENDTHRIFT

Balance
The pig is a Yin animal that exemplifies the Yin principles of peace, rest and harmony. On the whole, therefore, pigs are well-balanced people. Their lives will not suffer from the ups and downs typical of the more unbalanced animal signs such as the dragon and the horse. Indeed, the Chinese astrological symbol for the pig is a set of balanced scales.

TEN PIG DISLIKES
1. ARGUMENTS
2. BEING DECEITFUL
3. INHOSPITABLE PEOPLE
4. LIVING BY THEIR WITS ALONE
5. TO FEEL CONFUSED
6. MAKING DIFFICULT DECISIONS ALONE
7. POSSESSIVE PEOPLE
8. NOT KNOWING WHERE THEY STAND
9. TO BE REPROACHED
10. TO FALL OUT WITH FRIENDS